Would You Rather Christmas! Edition

Canggu Publishing

© Copyright 2019 - All rights reserved.

The content contained within this book may not be reproduced, duplicated or transmitted without direct written permission from the author or the publisher. Under no circumstances will any blame or legal responsibility be held against the publisher, or author, for any damages, reparation, or monetary loss due to the information contained within this book. Either directly or indirectly. You are responsible for your own choices, actions, and results.

Legal Notice:
This book is copyright protected. This book is only for personal use. You cannot amend, distribute, sell, use, quote or paraphrase any part, or the content within this book,
without the consent of the author or publisher.

Disclaimer Notice:
Please note the information contained within this document is for educational and entertainment purposes only. All effort has been executed to present accurate, up to date, and reliable, complete information. No warranties of any kind are declared or implied. Readers acknowledge that the author is not engaging in the rendering of legal, financial, medical or professional advice.

The content within this book has been derived
from various sources. Please consult a licensed professional before attempting any techniques outlined in this book.

By reading this document, the reader agrees that under no circumstances is the author responsible for any losses, direct or indirect, which are incurred as a result of the use of the information contained within this document, including, but not limited to, — errors, omissions, or inaccuracies.

How To Play ...

1) Have two or more people around (the more the better).

2) The person holding the book asks the question and the person listening HAS to answer one of the two options (no skipping).

3) Take turns asking questions (Don't keep the book to yourself).

4) That's it, have fun!

1

WOULD YOU RATHER...

Be able to turn into a reindeer on command but your nose will be red forever

or

Be able to fly but you'll have to wear Santa's red suite for ever?

2

WOULD YOU RATHER...

Swim in a pool full of Eggnog

or

Eat your way out of a house made of candy cane?

3

WOULD YOU RATHER...

Get to open all of your presents but a day after Christmas

or

Open all of them but lose one on Christmas Day and you don't get to choose which one it will be?

4

WOULD YOU RATHER...

Visit the most incredible toy store but not be able to buy anything

or

Visit a one dollar toy store and get to pick whatever you want?

5

WOULD YOU RATHER...

Have a stocking full of bouncy balls you can play with for days

or

A stocking full of rubber spiders you can scare countless people with?

6

WOULD YOU RATHER...

Get praised by your classmates for baking the best cupcakes but not get to eat any yourself

or

Keep them all for yourself and get no praise?

7

WOULD YOU RATHER...

Have to sing Christmas songs in a very busy street

or

Sing them in the church choir?

8

WOULD YOU RATHER...

Have to remove snow from the front of your house the month of Christmas

or

Have no snow at all?

9

WOULD YOU RATHER...

Have your hair like the bristles of a Christmas tree

or

Have Christmas balls hanging from your ears?

10

WOULD YOU RATHER...

Have Christmas on repeat for the rest of time

or

Erase Christmas forever?

11

WOULD YOU RATHER...

Have a very sunny Christmas day like in Australia

or

A very snowy one like in Switzerland?

12

WOULD YOU RATHER...

Find your stocking full of quarters on Christmas day

or

Get no gifts at all?

13

WOULD YOU RATHER...

Have to read all the letters sent to Santa from kids

or

Help Santa wrap all of the gifts?

14

WOULD YOU RATHER...

Have to sing Christmas carols every time you want to speak

or

Dress like Santa every time you want to go out of home?

15

WOULD YOU RATHER...

Have to wear Christmas ornaments all over your body like a walking Christmas tree

or

Have noisy jingle bells attached to each limb?

16

WOULD YOU RATHER...

Only eat turkey for the week of Christmas and get to drink anything

or

Only drink water and get to eat anything?

17

WOULD YOU RATHER...

Have no chores during Christmas time

or

No homework/exams leading up to Christmas?

18

WOULD YOU RATHER...

Become friends with Santa Claus

or

Best friends with the Grinch?

19

WOULD YOU RATHER...

Have a snowy Christmas but always get sick in the cold

or

Have no snow and never get sick?

20

WOULD YOU RATHER...

Watch 'The Elf' twenty times back to back

or

Never watch a Christmas movie ever again?

21

WOULD YOU RATHER...

Have all your classmates throw snowballs at you for an hour straight

or

Spend a week working on a Christmas tree farm?

22

WOULD YOU RATHER...

Be given five extra Christmas gifts

or

Give one gift to someone who didn't get any gifts?

23

WOULD YOU RATHER...

Get tickets to a concert of a band you don't like in your Christmas stocking

or

Get to give a stocking full of coal to someone you dislike?

24

WOULD YOU RATHER...

Get the gift you always wanted but have to give it away a month later

or

Get an average gift but be able to keep it forever?

25

WOULD YOU RATHER...

Have reindeer antlers grow on your head every time you tell a lie

or

Have your belly grow like Santa's every time you tell a lie?

26

WOULD YOU RATHER...

Take a trip to the North Pole and see Santa and the elves

or

Travel to an exotic beach in the Caribbean for a month?

27

WOULD YOU RATHER...

Be in a snowball fight in your neighborhood

or

Make a huge snowman with all your neighbors?

28

WOULD YOU RATHER...

Make Christmas cookies that taste like turkey

or

Make a turkey that tastes like Christmas cookies?

29

WOULD YOU RATHER...

Have a Christmas carol stuck in your head for a whole year

or

Say ho-ho-ho like Santa does every time you laugh for a month?

30

WOULD YOU RATHER...

Be able to celebrate Christmas twice a year

or

Be able to celebrate your birthday twice a year?

31

WOULD YOU RATHER...

Celebrate Christmas with your five favorite family members

or

Have your house full of fifty friends and family during Christmas?

32

WOULD YOU RATHER...

Have unlimited leftover turkey in the fridge all year

or

Have unlimited leftover eggnog?

33

WOULD YOU RATHER...

Wear a wooly Christmas knitted sweater all Summer

or

Have a carrot for a nose for a week?

34

WOULD YOU RATHER...

Be the only one in the room who didn't get a Christmas gift

or

Be the only one in the room who did get one?

35

WOULD YOU RATHER...

Only get socks from everyone as a Christmas present

or

Only get underwear?

36

WOULD YOU RATHER...

Witness when Santa comes down the chimney

or

Witness when the sleigh is flying away in the sky?

37

WOULD YOU RATHER...

Have gravy breath for a month

or

Give up Christmas desserts forever?

38

WOULD YOU RATHER...

Win the lottery but erase Christmas forever

or

Celebrate Christmas every year but with no money?

39

WOULD YOU RATHER...

Have cold weather for Christmas with no heating

or

Hot weather for Christmas with no air conditioning?

40

WOULD YOU RATHER...

Get to listen to Santa's reindeer sing Christmas carols

or

Listen to the Grinch sing Christmas carols?

41

WOULD YOU RATHER...

Freeze time so Christmas lasts longer

or

Freeze summer time to enjoy the weather for longer?

42

WOULD YOU RATHER...

Not be able to wake up on Christmas Day because you are so sleepy that you can't even open your eyes

or

Have insomnia for one week before Christmas Day?

43

WOULD YOU RATHER...

Have your head with the body of Santa

or

Have your head with the body of a snowman?

44

WOULD YOU RATHER...

Brush your teeth with gravy

or

Wash your hair with hot cocoa?

45

WOULD YOU RATHER...

Eat your cereal with buttered rum instead of milk

or

With cider instead of milk?

46

WOULD YOU RATHER...

Live in a gingerbread palace

or

Live in the North Pole next to Santa?

47

WOULD YOU RATHER...

Be able to relive a past
Christmas holiday again

or

Be able to travel to a future
Christmas holiday?

48

WOULD YOU RATHER...

Spend Christmas with all your family

or

With one celebrity of your choice?

49

WOULD YOU RATHER...

Have to cook Christmas dinner by yourself

or

Have to do the dishes after the Christmas dinner all by yourself?

50

WOULD YOU RATHER...

Get stuck in an elevator for Christmas Eve by yourself

or

Get stuck in an airport due to bad weather with other strangers?

51

WOULD YOU RATHER...

Live a Christmas in the year 1500

or

In the year 2500?

52

WOULD YOU RATHER...

Travel to another destination of your choice and celebrate Christmas with just your family members without Christmas food

or

Stay home and celebrate with everyone you usually do with all the classic Christmas food?

53

WOULD YOU RATHER...

Have candy cane arms that you can constantly suck on

or

Gingerbread legs that grow back after you eat them?

54

WOULD YOU RATHER...

Leave Christmas decorations all year round

or

Never be able to put them up again?

55

WOULD YOU RATHER...

Be the only house on the street with decorated lights

or

Be the only house on the street with no lights?

56

WOULD YOU RATHER...

A broken front yard because the Reindeers crashed

or

Squished presents because Santa fell on them?

57

WOULD YOU RATHER...

Read a five hundred page book about Christmas traditions in countries where it's celebrated

or

Write a hundred page essay about Christmas?

58

WOULD YOU RATHER...

Accidentally sit on a very sharp candy cane

or

Cut the turkey to find out that the center is uncooked?

59

WOULD YOU RATHER...

Decorate your Christmas tree with tennis balls and cob webs

or

Decorate it with embarrassing photos of yourself hanging from it?

60

WOULD YOU RATHER...

Replace Santa's reindeer with flying kangaroos

or

Replace Santa's sleigh with flying polar bears?

61

WOULD YOU RATHER...

Listen to a rock version of Jingle Bells at the mall for two hours

or

Listen to silly Christmas jokes at the mall for four hours?

62

WOULD YOU RATHER...

Walk barefoot on snow for a mile to get the gift you always wanted for Christmas

or

Stay in the freezing cold pond for twenty minutes to get the present?

63

WOULD YOU RATHER...

Knit ten sweaters to give them away as Christmas presents

or

Wear underwear made of Santa's beard hair for a day and not have to knit anything?

64

WOULD YOU RATHER...

Be covered head to toe in cranberry sauce for two hours

or

Have to carry around heavy antlers on the top of your head all day?

65

WOULD YOU RATHER...

Spend a day making Christmas cookies and surprise the entire neighborhood with them

or

Spend the day having a snowball fight and watching movies with the neighborhood?

66

WOULD YOU RATHER...

Lose your luggage at the airport after a trip

or

Lose all the gifts you bought at the mall?

67

WOULD YOU RATHER...

Have a high squeaky voice like an elf

or

Have a husky and deep voice like Santa?

68

WOULD YOU RATHER...

Eat mashed potatoes flavored fruitcake

or

Eat fruitcake flavored mashed potatoes?

69

WOULD YOU RATHER...

Turn into a cheerful snowman on Christmas night every year

or

Turn into an evil elf?

70

WOULD YOU RATHER...

Be Santa's best friend and get to talk to him about anything you want

or

Rudolph's best friend and be able to fly any where you want?

71

WOULD YOU RATHER...

Know how to beautifully wrap presents

or

Know how to beautifully decorate a Christmas tree?

72

WOULD YOU RATHER...

Have an elf's body for a day

or

A reindeer's hooves for your hands and feet for a day?

73

WOULD YOU RATHER...

Go to school and forget that you were meant to be wearing Christmas clothes and everyone else is

or

Wear Christmas clothes to school and be the only one doing so?

74

WOULD YOU RATHER...

Paint your house with green and red

or

Wear green and red clothes for an entire month?

75

WOULD YOU RATHER...

Write five hundred individual Christmas cards

or

Personally deliver five hundred Christmas cards and see the children's faces light when you give it to them?

76

WOULD YOU RATHER...

Bake and decorate 1000 Christmas cookies

or

Have no dessert for Christmas?

77

WOULD YOU RATHER...

Learn the languages of the reindeer and be able to speak to them

or

Speak an elf language that no one except the elves understand?

78

WOULD YOU RATHER...

Have no snow days and lots of presents

or

Lots of snow days and a few presents?

79

WOULD YOU RATHER...

Give up Christmas presents next year

or

Give up birthday presents next year?

80

WOULD YOU RATHER...

Be wrapped like a present for a day with only your head and legs outside the box

or

Wear a mistletoe on top of your head for a week?

81

WOULD YOU RATHER...

Ride on Rudolph the Red Nose Reindeer

or

Sit next to Santa on his sleigh?

82

WOULD YOU RATHER...

Have to wait an extra week for Christmas to arrive this year

or

Have a week less holidays this break and Christmas is still on the 25th?

83

WOULD YOU RATHER...

Have small and short hands like an elf

or

Have skinny, long and hairy hands like the Grinch?

84

WOULD YOU RATHER...

Have to shovel snow from your driveway on Christmas morning to get your gifts

or

Untangle one hundred Christmas lights before you can open your gifts?

85

WOULD YOU RATHER...

A new car you get to choose for you family for Christmas

or

A brand new boat?

86

WOULD YOU RATHER...

Have to drink a gallon of punch

or

Drink a gallon of cider?

87

WOULD YOU RATHER...

Help to prepare a great
Christmas dinner at home

or

Help to decorate the house
with Christmas ornaments?

88

WOULD YOU RATHER...

Wear a Halloween costume on Christmas day

or

Dress like Santa on Halloween?

89

WOULD YOU RATHER...

Find a puppy in your stocking

or

A thousand dollar gift voucher to Walmart?

90

WOULD YOU RATHER...

Have your Christmas cookies burnt in the oven

or

Have a very salty turkey?

91

WOULD YOU RATHER...

Only be able to decorate the exterior of your house

or

Only the interior of your house?

92

WOULD YOU RATHER...

Have the power to make it snow whenever you want

or

Be able to melt snow whenever you want?

93

WOULD YOU RATHER...

Win a free Christmas trip to a place you don't want to go

or

Not go on holiday at all?

94

WOULD YOU RATHER...

Drop the main course for the Christmas dinner

or

Your most prized present in turn damaging it?

95

WOULD YOU RATHER...

Play in a snowball fight with balls the size of a basketball ball

or

Build a snowman the size of a two floor building?

96

WOULD YOU RATHER...

Help bake the world's biggest Gingerbread man

or

Decorate the world's tallest Christmas tree?

97

WOULD YOU RATHER...

Not know what you're getting for presents each year and you're surprised

or

Know in advance and there's no surprise?

98

WOULD YOU RATHER...

Get your stocking full of small expensive gifts

or

A lot of big but not so expensive gifts?

99

WOULD YOU RATHER...

Add a mistletoe to the top of your Christmas tree that can blink cool colors and dance to music

or

A talking star that can sing and quote movies?

100

WOULD YOU RATHER...

Use Santa's red sack as your backpack for school all year

or

Always carry all books in your hands?

101

WOULD YOU RATHER...

Take a bath in gravy

or

Have a shower with eggnog instead of water?

102

WOULD YOU RATHER...

Live with the elves and help them build some toys

or

Sit with Santa and help him deliver some toys?

103

WOULD YOU RATHER...

Listen to Christmas carols on repeat for 24 hours

or

Never hear one again for the rest of your life?

104

WOULD YOU RATHER...

Have a perfume that smells like stuffing

or

Cook a turkey that smells like perfume?

105

WOULD YOU RATHER...

Have to wear a fake itchy beard all of Christmas

or

An itchy Santa hat?

106

WOULD YOU RATHER...

Eat average food on Christmas that is cooked to perfection

or

Get to eat your favorite meal but it's slightly burnt?

107

WOULD YOU RATHER...

Drink and eat the milk and cookies if you were Santa

or

Have McDonald's and a milkshake instead?

108

WOULD YOU RATHER...

Be in the movie 'The Grinch'

or

Be in the movie 'Home Alone'?

109

WOULD YOU RATHER...

Watch the Christmas parade on TV

or

Be part of the parade with everyone else?

110

WOULD YOU RATHER...

Go to bed early on Christmas Eve but open a present

or

Stay up late and not be able to open any presents till the morning?

111

WOULD YOU RATHER...

Decorate your Christmas tree only with lego made ornaments

or

Leave the tree naked?

112

WOULD YOU RATHER...

Receive all your presents without any names on them

or

Forget what everything is called Christmas related?

113

WOULD YOU RATHER...

Go to the beach on New Year's Day dressed as Santa

or

Dress up as an elf for the first day of school?

114

WOULD YOU RATHER...

Be hired as an elf for a month

or

Be hired as a sleigh engineer?

115

WOULD YOU RATHER...

Have unlimited eggnog to drink

or

Unlimited mulled wine to drink?

116

WOULD YOU RATHER...

Make all Christmas presents with your own hands

or

Buy all the presents and not have to make any?

117

WOULD YOU RATHER...

Wear the same Christmas sweater every day for the next three months

or

Wear funny Christmas socks for the whole year?

118

WOULD YOU RATHER...

Trip backwards in the snow while drinking hot chocolate

or

Trip forwards on ice while holding a bowl of punch?

119

WOULD YOU RATHER...

Sing Jingle Bells live on Facebook for five minutes

or

Sing Christmas carols at your school entrance for an hour ?

120

WOULD YOU RATHER...

Fit baby marshmallows in each ear

or

In each nostril?

121

WOULD YOU RATHER...

Get dropped off to school in a sled pulled by reindeer

or

On the back of an individual reindeer?

122

WOULD YOU RATHER...

Have your head on an elf body

or

An elf's head and your body?

123

WOULD YOU RATHER...

Burn your tongue a little eating a fresh cookie from the oven

or

Get an ice freeze drinking a really cold cider?

124

WOULD YOU RATHER...

See Santa wear your regular clothes

or

See a reindeer wear your underwear?

125

WOULD YOU RATHER...

Rather see Santa giving out presents in shorts and shirt like he does in the south

or

See him wearing a green suit like he used to before it was red?

126

WOULD YOU RATHER...

Have a snowball fight with your friends

or

Enjoy a nice Christmas meal with all of them instead?

127

WOULD YOU RATHER...

Be as short as an elf

or

As big as Santa?

128

WOULD YOU RATHER...

Teach your dog how to make snowballs

or

Teach it how to unwrap presents?

129

WOULD YOU RATHER...

Create a snowman with bare hands

or

Create a snow angel in shorts and a tee?

130

WOULD YOU RATHER...

Wrap presents for two hours

or

Spend two hours setting up the Christmas tree?

131

WOULD YOU RATHER...

Only eat gingerbread men all Christmas Day and nothing else

or

Drink Hot Chocolate all Christmas Day and have nothing else?

132

WOULD YOU RATHER...

Have an elf as a family member

or

A reindeer as a pet?

133

WOULD YOU RATHER...

It rained eggnog on Christmas

or

It rained marshmallows on Christmas?

134

WOULD YOU RATHER...

Wake up on Christmas day to realize that it's actually the middle of August

or

Wake up on December 26th and realize you just missed Christmas day because you were sleeping?

www.ingramcontent.com/pod-product-compliance
Lightning Source LLC
Chambersburg PA
CBHW070945080526
44587CB00015B/2227